Future of Humankind

Western Civilization Versus Islam

Dr. Shah Ebadur Rahman Neshat

Former professor of English
Ummul Qura University, Makkah

Time has arrived when the Message of the Prophet Muhammad (blessings and peace be on him) is presented to mankind on the strength of evidence and rational appeal.

Shah Waliyullah Dehlawi
Preface, Hujjatullahil Baligha
(Shah Waliyullah awr Unke Tajdidi Karname
by Hakeem Mahmood Ahmad Zafar, p. 108)

For

Maryam

My first grandchild

(May Allah be her guardian and protector)

Contents

In the name of Allah, the Beneficent, the Merciful

PREFACE

West versus Islam is a familiar topic which has been visited from different perspectives by different authors. The present work brings the two face to face against each other on one specific question: which of the two can best serve and protect the future of humankind?

Instead of attempting a comparison between Christianity and Islam, or between Western civilization and Islamic civilization, which would have been more logical, the present topic seemed more realistic to me. The West does not represent Christianity and Islamic civilization is not represented by any Islamic nation in the present world. However, Western civilization and Islam are realities that have asserted their entities in history and claim in their own ways that they could lead humanity to an ideal future of happiness, peace and prosperity.

If Western civilization can justifiably claim to have brought to humankind material affluence and prosperity in the present age, Islam can claim equally justifiably that it created a majestic empire and a glorious civilization in the recent past and can do so in the future. If we allow them further to show each other's fault lines, Western civilization points out that Islam is not capable of providing humankind with the rich scientific and technological facilities that it has done, and Islam retorts that it already established a materially rich civilization fully backed by the moral and spiritual excellence that Western civilization miserably lacks. These claims and counter claims provide an interesting setting for a comparison between the two when we evaluate them as contestants on the issue of the future of humankind. For if Western civilization criticizes Islam for dividing humanity on the basis of religion, Islam accuses Western civilization that it has thrust upon humankind an imminent danger of the annihilation of the very human race, *Homo sapiens*, that has created it. Islam asserts that if the world is led by Western civilization, it will in near future be inhabited by a generation of beings (a further advanced evolutionary species that we could call *superhumans*) that will either enslave *Homo sapiens* or eliminate it from the face of the earth. It is a very serious charge, but as it is affirmed by evolutionists and scientists themselves, it deserves serious attention.

Thus, it is a valid question to ask: Which of the two, Western civilization or Islam, can protect the future of humankind and honor their right to exist, live in peace and strive for prosperity? This book will attempt to investigate this very question.

It is true that Western civilization is now a global phenomenon which has revolutionized all spheres of knowledge and all aspects of life with its principles and teachings which are essentially materialistic. However, in this study I have narrowed down the sphere of investigation by delimiting the discussion to a specific question which concerns the effect of Western civilization on the ultimate fate of humankind – the issue of their very existence.

I have two classes of readers in mind: one, the Muslims who need to know how radically the world has changed under the influence of science and technology in recent years and how their responsibility of establishing the relevance of Islam in it demands new preparedness; and two, the secular readers, Muslims as well as non-Muslims, who need to know that the teachings of Islam are scientific in essence, contemporary in spirit and practically fully capable of carving out an ideal human society. It is in the interest of both that they break the barriers, for if they do so they may reach out to each other for sharing experiences which is so urgently needed to save the world from the disaster that it is currently faced with.

Shah Ebadur Rahman Neshat

Delhi, May 14, 2020

INTRODUCTION

Aim and scope of the Study

Modern Western civilization, with the support of science and technology, has revolutionized the whole world. It has reduced the world into a global village and, after taming the wild forces of nature on earth, is now flying high up in the skies to conquer the space. This civilization is acknowledged as the most powerful phenomenon in history which stands out as the only power that could ensure a most secure and prosperous future for humankind.

In this situation it is truly disconcerting that the very ability of Western civilization to lead humankind to a safe and secure future is being seriously questioned now. Informed people are beset by anxiety and confusion about the nature, capability and intent of Western civilization and want to understand whether it is leading the human race towards a glorious future or to annihilation. It is apprehended that Western civilization may turn rogue and destroy the very human race that has created it. This apprehension is very serious but as this possibility is in the vey gene of this civilization, as we will see later, and as the protagonists of this civilization themselves are affirming it, it needs to be closely looked at in the light of the philosophical bases and practical inclinations of Western civilization. We will investigate this issue in this study and try to determine what the situation is.

But this question is not so simple and cannot be studied out of context. Even if we come to the conclusion that there is truth in this apprehension, we will still have to determine what the way out of this situation could be. If not Western civilization, then what? What is the alternative that will fill the gap? What is it that can guide humankind to a happy and safe future and is also free from the lacunae of Western civilization? Is there a better option?

Can we consider Religion as an alternative to modern Western civilization? We can, but we face here a difficulty at the very outset. Religions differ in their perception of a happy worldly life. Some religions altogether reject the importance of worldly life by overemphasizing the issue of redemption in the afterlife and cannot contest with modern civilization which has won the hearts of the people by providing material affluence to them. Some others divide humankind on the basis of race, caste and gender and grant superior status only to a privileged class in the society. Quite naturally, such religions also cannot win back humankind to their side. Obviously, religions cannot form a common platform to compete with Western civilization.

The other option is that we pick up just one religion that claims to guarantee an ideal future for humankind, including all material attainments that Western civilization offers, and is not at all threatening to them in any way. From this point of view Islam is an option. It claims that it has a framework of development and progress that can compete with that of Western civilization at the material and intellectual levels and could also provide moral and spiritual guidelines to humankind which are completely ignored in Western civilization. We will therefore give Islam a chance in this study as against Western civilization and see what model of an ideal future for humankind it provides and how practical it is.

So, the objective of this study will be to draw a comparison between Western civilization and Islam as protagonists of the future of humankind and see which of the two safeguards it best.

Organization of the Study

Chapter One will provide definition of key terms used in the study so that the readers understand them in the specific context in which they are used. Chapter Two will focus the contributions of Western civilization in regard to the formation of a prosperous future for humankind. Chapter Three will look into the claims of Islam for constructing an ideal future for humankind; we will also discuss its practical achievements in this regard in the recent past. For both, the same parameters of comparison will be adopted. Chapter Four will be a summary of the differences between Western civilization and

Islam that emerge from the above discussion. Chapter Five will be the conclusion that will sum up the discussion.

ONE

DEFINITION OF KEY TERMS

In this study we will concentrate on three main terms: Humankind, Western civilization and Islam. We will in this section establish their clear definitions so that they are understood in the perspective in which they are used in this study.

1. Humankind

As we are discussing in this study the future of humankind, we must analyze the true nature of humans as closely as possible so as to be able to judge which model, Western civilization's or Islam's, will suit them best. Humans possess several in-built faculties which are complementary to each other and determine their nature and character. They have first a "physical" self, a body, which helps them fulfill their mundane obligations and makes it possible for them to procreate. Second, they have "intelligence," a rational faculty, with which they analyze challenges, explore possibilities and keep on moving forward on the road of progress. Third, they also have a "moral" sense, often referred to as "conscience," which tells them what is right and what is wrong; they are satisfied when their moral urge is fulfilled and feel guilty when it is defied. And the fourth is the "spiritual" faculty which is a very refined sensibility in humans inspiring them to search for their Creator and connect to Him. These four different faculties form a beautiful synthesis in humans which is essentially human-specific and is not found in any other creature on earth. Thus, only that framework of a happy life and civilizational progress will satisfy humankind that could cater for their needs at all these levels – physical, rational, moral and spiritual. It is on these parameters that we will evaluate both Western civilization and Islam.

A clarification may be helpful here. The framework that we have established above does not unduly favor religion by including spirituality as a parameter. We should remember that spirituality is fully recognized as a natural faculty in humankind. Karen Armstrong, who identifies herself as an atheist in her famous book *A History of God*, comments: "Yet my study of the history of religion has revealed that human beings are spiritual animals. Indeed, there is a case for arguing that *Homo sapiens* is also *Homo religious*."[1] Also, most countries recognize the importance of religion and the majority of the world population consists of believers of one religion or another.

---

[1] Karen Armstrong, *A History of God* (New York: Ballantine Books, 1993), p. xix.

2. Western Civilization

By Western civilization we mean here the civilization that was born as a result of the Renaissance in Europe around the fifteenth century. Equipped with science and technology, it has grown now into a gigantic phenomenon and stands out as truly unparalleled in the history of humankind.

The first remarkable characteristic of this civilization is its insistence on the freedom of thought due to which it had a direct clash with the Catholic Church as soon as it was born in Europe. It supported the free investigative spirit of science and challenged the irrational teachings of religion. As history tells us, the church decided to crush the questioning spirit of science and punished its protagonists by forcing them to apologize, or drink the deadly poison, or undergo other forms of punishment recommended by the Inquisition, or run for life to safe places. This clash became bloody, but ultimately science won the battle. As a result, science freed itself completely from the dominance of religion and pursued explorative projects in different fields with the help of a new tool – the Experimental Method. Thus, the Western civilization that grew in this situation in Europe became purely materialist and rational and denied the tenets of religion as they could not be proved by scientific investigation. It thus fully relied on science and technology and chose the material field for its ventures.

It is to be noted that in Western civilization the focus is fully on material development intended to serve humans at the physical level. It surely acknowledges the intellectual faculty in humankind and in fact makes maximum use of it for developmental purposes, but the intellectual faculty, which is higher in essence than the physical faculty, is obliged to stoop down and serve human civilization at the physical and material level. If we carefully look at the long list of the innovations of Western civilization, past and present, we will notice that most of them are, in form or spirit, meant to make human life physically more comfortable. For example, the achievements in the areas of medicine, transportation, travel, banking, administration, government formation, economic systems, individual freedom, social liberty, and we name it, are ventures at the material level for the fulfillment of physical needs of humans. It is true that Western civilization has now revolutionized all aspects of life, but in all areas of its influence its impact is essentially materialistic. Liberalism in philosophy, or capitalism in economy, or democracy in politics, or reformation and humanism in religion – all these are essentially Western civilization's desire to promote physical and material growth and grant morality and spirituality (and religion that espouses them) only a small corner outside the realm of active life. Moral values in Western civilization are what the majority approves of, and spirituality for it is strictly for the internal support that humans need from time to time for making an adjustment to the ups and downs of life, not because it is an essential reality.

3. Islam

Islam is a strong contestant of Western Civilization claiming that it can provide a framework for the over-all progress and prosperity of humankind which is comprehensive, balanced and safe and is fully suited to human nature. It also claims that it created an ideal civilization in the near past which testifies that its blue print for progress is fully practicable.

Islam teaches that humans are 'created,' signaling that this universe has a creator, called God in general and Allah in Islam, Who has created them with a mission to lead a purposeful life in accordance with His teachings and make the world an ideal place for all to live. As the afterlife is a reality in Islam, so is the mundane world which is directly connected to how humans shall fare in the afterlife. As programmed by God, human beings are appointed as God's vicegerent (*khalifa)* who are supposed to establish peace and justice on earth for fellow beings by introducing in the practical form the divine injunctions. The Prophet of Islam, peace and blessings be on him, is reported to have said to one of his companions, 'Adi, son of Hatim Tai:[2] When Allah shall establish the Message

---

[2] This Hatim Tai is the same legendary figure who is known for his extraordinary generosity and hospitality. He died before the revelation of Islam. His son 'Adi accepted Islam in the days of the Prophet.

with which I am sent to the world, a woman from San'a [in Yemen] will travel to Makkah [in Saudi Arabia] by her camel and will have no fear that somebody might hurt her [in the way] finding her alone and helpless.[3]

Islam presents clear guidelines and a comprehensive structure for operational purposes and for maintaining law and order at all levels: personal, social, national and international, which are enunciated in the Qur'an and Hadith. In the world that Islam creates, humans will not be plagued by racial, tribal, color or gender discrimination. Right to life, property, education and human dignity will be granted to all. The rulers will have their administrative power, but a common man, Muslim or non-Muslim, man or woman, rich or poor, will also enjoy a right to live in peace and dignity and, if challenged, seek justice in the Islamic court against the offender, be he the ruler. Instances are galore when the citizens used this right against the *Khalifa* of an Islamic state. An Islamic state will fully protect its non-Muslim citizens by granting them generous provisions for practicing their individual, social, economic and religious rights; they will be free to practice their Personal Law and form their own

---

[3] The hadith runs like this: The Prophet of Allah said, 'Adi! Have you been to Al-Hira?' 'Adi replied: I haven't been to it, but I was informed about it.' Thereupon the Prophet said: "If you live for a long time, you will certainly see that a woman riding a camel will travel alone from Al-Hira to Makkah and perform the Tawaf of the Ka'ba [after reaching there safely], and [in that journey] she will fear none but Allah." (*Sahih Al Bukhari*, Hadith No. 3595)

religious courts under their religious leaders.[4] The Qur`an and Hadith duly enunciate the rules that govern international relations of a Muslim state with other states, Muslim or non-Muslim.

Islam endorses that humans are gifted with a 'physical' self which has to be fully attended and nurtured in consonance with their 'spiritual' self. It attaches due importance to the material environment in which humans have to perform. It also recognizes the faculty of "reason" as a divine gift. It acknowledges that knowledge gained through five sensory means – seeing, hearing, smelling, tasting, and touching – are reliable and that "reason" can take humans beyond the realm of sensory faculties which should be duly recognized. But, as it says, where reason fails to assert itself, humans would need help from "revelation" (*wahiy*) which is a guidance from the Providence. For Muslims the message is clear that the function of "reason" is to discover the cause-and-effect relations operating in nature, and the function of "revelation" is to discover the Creator of those causal relations. Islam asserts that all faculties inherent in the nature of humans are positive and can help them live an ideal life on earth and qualify for God's benevolence in the hereafter. It is therefore neither against rationality nor scientific investigation and experimentation. It, in fact, makes its followers responsible for ensuring the physical wellbeing and material progress of humans and promises divine reward if they sincerely do so.

Now we are ready to take up the main question and see what will be the future of humankind under modern Western civilization and how it will be if they take guidelines from Islam.

TWO

FUTURE OF HUMANKIND UNDER WESTERN CIVILIZATION

In this section we will investigate what will be the future of humankind, *Homo sapiens*, if they follow Western civilization.

In order to find an answer to this question, we will have to begin with the origins of life on earth, for, as the evolutionists hold, the Law of Nature that created life on earth and is responsible for its evolution up to the present stage, will also control its evolution in the future. It is therefore in the story of their evolution in the past that we will discover the prospect of their future. It is to be clarified here that Western civilization subscribes to the theory of evolution for the emergence of life on earth. Will and Ariel Durant, for instance, testify that "the first biological lesson of history is that life is competition" and "the second biological lesson of history is that life is selection."[5] It will also help us if we remind ourselves once again that Western civilization has achieved its present status with the help of science and technology to the extent that they have almost become synonyms for it.

---

[5] Will and Ariel Durant, *The Lessons of History* (New York: Simon & Schuster Paperback, 1996), p, 19.

A. The Origins of Life

Yuval Noah Harari in his famous book *Sapiens: A Brief History of Humankind,* narrates the story of the origins of humankind on earth and says that 13. 5 billion years ago there came into existence in the space our planet Earth which took again billions of years to cool down enabling the emergence of life on it in the initial form 3. 8 billion years ago. Then life in different forms appeared which, under the process of natural selection, perished and was born again in other forms and thus continued the caravan of life on earth. The living creatures which succeeded in adapting to the environment survived and through the process of natural selection kept on improving. As Atul Jalan puts it, this process is "is called natural selection because it happens on its own and cannot be influenced."[6]

Humans, popularly called *Homo sapiens* by evolutionists which means 'creature with intelligence,' proved fortunate as they excelled other creatures in adaptability and emerged as the most advanced and therefore most powerful species on the scale of the survival of the fittest.

But human progress in evolution remained very slow. Humans freed their hands by learning to walk on foot,

---

[6] Atul Jalan, *Where Will Man Take Us?* (Gurgaon: Penguin Random House, 2019), p. 54.

advanced from the stage of hunter-gatherer to that of agriculturist and keeper of herds, and discovered fire, wheel and use of sea routes, but it took them millions of years in achieving these feats which were in fact, rather humble in terms of time. It is important to remember that up to this point changes that occurred in humans at the physical level were governed by natural selection.

But 70,000 years ago, a big change took place in humans which is referred to as Cognitive Revolution.[7] It marks a turning point in human history as at this stage they freed themselves from their dependence on natural selection and learned to use their intelligence to solve their problems. As a result, they embarked on progress through discoveries and innovations that they had never dreamed of. It is true that the cause of this cognitive revolution is not yet known, but with the help of it humans created a new world for themselves and kept on improving it by 'intelligent design,' the rational ability created in man by cognitive revolution. Now it is humans who control the world and are the conqueror of natural resources and master of other creatures that inhabit the earth. Their closest cousin, the chimpanzee, finds now a place in the zoo and circus while they fly in the plane, eat at luxury restaurants and pay for their commercial transactions through Paytm.

---

[7] Yuval Noah Harari, *Sapiens: A Brief History of Humankind* (London: Vintage, 2011), p. 23. Harari mentions on the same page that the cause of cognitive revolution in humans is not yet known.

Humans also excelled other creatures in the use of language. Formerly, human language was limited to physical gestures and voice signals, but later it acquired, besides other distinguishing features, the quality of displacement: they were now able to talk about things that were not present on the scene (such as an incident from the past), things that they had never seen (angels, paradise, hell), new concepts (socialism, capitalism), or anything that mattered.

Humans, or *Homo sapiens*, slowly settled down at the banks of rivers for the availability of water and fish and learned cultivation and domestication of animals; they especially kept dogs that provided protection to them and their herds. This led them to Agricultural Revolution some 12,000 years ago which obliged them to settle down at convenient places minimizing nomadic wanderings.

Slowly their habitations grew in size, from small tribal settlements to large villages, and then it was only a matter of time that community needs generated small business units which led to the development of barter system and then to import and export in due course of time. The growth of language, especially the acquisition of writing system, helped them in formalizing commercial contracts and keeping records.

Homo sapiens further organized themselves and developed religious, moral and cultural values which provided new bases for amicable relationship among different groups and promoted mutual visits and exchanges. Besides other advantages of it, such contacts enriched human experience leading to Scientific Revolution roughly 500 years ago which introduced humans to immense opportunities for exploration. Technology now came to the aid of humans which reduced distance and removed barriers at all levels. With the development of roads, railways, ships and airplanes, people started traveling to far off places for trade, education, medical facilities and in search of knowledge. New geographical boundaries of countries were established, various systems of government were adopted at different places, national and international laws were formulated and ultimately this large universe turned into a global village in which we live.

B. What Did Western Civilization Give to Humankind?

In this section we will look at the contributions of modern Western civilization and, for the sake of convenience, divide them under four headings: material, intellectual, moral and spiritual. This framework will help us judge how comprehensive these contributions are and how successfully they satisfy human needs in totality. We will evaluate the contributions of Islam on the same parameters that we use here for Western civilization.

Contributions of Western Civilization at the Material Level

As Western civilization is based on science and technology and relies on inductive logic and experimental method for verification of a proposition, it naturally works with physical entities that could be ascertained by sensory faculties and checked and verified by experimentation. That is why it has been able to make most of its prize achievements at the material level.

By nature, the physical needs of humans are always immediate and urgent. Humans, for example, attach great importance to food, water, shelter and protection from threats to life, which are all physical realities, and it is at this level that Western civilization offered its valuable help to them. Yuval Noah Harari in his much-celebrated book *Homo Deus*, mentions three such phenomena - famine, plague, and war - that have been challenging humans at the physical level since time immemorial, but have now been greatly minimized by Western civilization. We will use Harari's format here for discussing the material contributions of Western civilization and consider its success in these three areas as reflective of its overall achievements. It is to be noted that this format has also been used by other scholars. Thomas R. Malthus, the famous economist of the 19th century, in his "Essay on Population" (1798), also identifies 'famine, pestilence and war' as three natural checks on the growth of population.[8] By concentrating on these areas we will be able to see the benevolent services that Western civilization has rendered for improving the quality of human life.

i.   Control of famine

Modern Western Civilization has achieved a remarkable success in controlling famine which used to kill humans at a very large scale. Drought, flood and other natural calamities created shortage of food due to which humans died helplessly in large numbers every now and then. In France, for example, 2. 8 million people died due to famine between 1692 and 1694 AD, which was 15 per cent of the total population of France. In Estonia in 1695, 20 per cent of the population died out of hunger, and in Finland in 1696 one-fourth to one-third of the total population perished due to famine. In Bengal during the British regime a serious famine broke out in 1769 which continued up to 1773 and killed 10 million people which was one-third of the total population.[9]

Modern civilization harnessed scientific research and technological aid in order to fight famine and succeeded in controlling it. As a result, it has not only increased the production of crops, fruit and vegetables tremendously by

---

[8] Will and Ariel Durant, pp. 21-22.

[9] Yuval Noah Harari, *Homo Deus: A Brief History of Tomorrow* (London: Vintage, 2017), p. 4.

using new machines, pesticide, irrigation facilities and high-quality seeds, but has also succeeded in preserving the surplus produce in warehouses for future use. It has also tremendously increased the production of meat and fish by developing chicken and animal farming and fisheries. Science has also helped in the growth of inorganic food items prepared without the help of traditional food ingredients, which are rich in health supporting supplements, perfectly suitable for human consumption and very tasteful. The well-known chain restaurant Burger King has very recently introduced a burger which tastes meaty but has been prepared by plant protein.[10] Such inorganic food items, as we can understand, have a tremendous potentiality to eradicate famine at any level.

The advanced means of transportation also plays a very vital role in reducing the burden of famine. If there is any such emergency in a particular country, food items can easily be rushed there from other countries in sufficient amount to meet the challenge. Harari comments on the present situation in these words: "There are no longer natural famines in the world; there are political famines. If people in Syria, Sudan and Somalia starve to death, it is because some politician wants them to."[11]

---

[10] *The Indian Express*, "Synthetic Biology," Delhi, 18 April, 2019, p. 15.
[11] Harari, *Homo Deus*, pp. 7-16.

It is to be noted that in the present age people are dying not due to shortage of food, but because they are overweight due to overeating. Harari makes an interesting observation that in 2010 AD about one million people died due to famine and malnutrition whereas in the same year three million people died of diseases caused by obesity due to overconsumption of food.[12] It is said that today's problem is not the shortage of food; it is obesity. People are now trying dozens of ways to eat less so as to keep their weight in control.[13]

ii. Control of Diseases

Western civilization has also been very successful in controlling diseases. Some fearsome diseases which created havoc in the past by killing humans in large numbers have been eradicated while others are put under control by discovering proper treatment for them. Plague, small pox, measles and such other contagious diseases which were considered utterly incurable in the past have been fully controlled now. The epidemic plague, known in history as Black Death, which spread in 1330 AD in Asia, Europe and South Africa, killed people somewhere between 75 million and

---

[12] Harari, *Homo Deus*, p. 6.

[13] COVID 19 is now challenging all these calculations. Newspapers are reporting that next year the number of starving people in the world will double due to the ravages of this disease. Only time will confirm or refute such predictions.

200 million. In France in the 20th century Spanish Flu killed half a million people in only a few months. This disease then spread to other countries: in India it killed 15 million, in Tahiti 14 percent of its population, and in the Congo 20 percent of the workers employed in the copper mines. These and other diseases kept on striking human habitations and turned them into virtual graveyards. But new research into the field, well supported by generous funding by private and public sources, has now changed the situation. The invention of proper medicines like antibiotics and vaccinations, advancement in surgery, improvement in health care and development of health consciousness in the general public have halted the spread of traditional diseases. It is a fact that new diseases, such as bird flu, swine flu, Ebola, Aids, and coronavirus are up in arms against humans, but the medical doctors and researchers seem to be alert and prepared to combat and control them.[14]

---

[14] Harari, *Homo Deus,* pp. 7-16. The claim of tremendous improvement in medical facilities in the present age is well acknowledged, but the war between nature and humans is really huge in which humans seem to be at a disadvantageous position. Recent research shows that the number of viruses in the air is much larger than even the number of the planets in the space. Humans hardly control the outbreak of one disease that the other attacks and keeps the world at its toes. The unbelievable growth in international travels on daily basis has further worsened the situation. While these lines are being written, the world is in the grip of coronavirus, COVID 19. The world will see how reliable is the present status of medical preparedness in controlling an emergency like this. What we know at present about this disease is that we do not know how to deal with it: social

iii.   Reducing the Possibility of War

War has been perhaps the most brutal enemy of humankind which allows the mighty to destroy the weak: it is most brutal because in it humans kill humans, unlike famine and epidemic which are natural catastrophes. Although it has been as old a phenomenon as human life on earth, in one form or another, the memory of recent wars is still fresh and creates an unprecedented anxiety and horror in our minds. In the First World War ten million people died, twenty-one million were injured and seventy thousand were reported as traceless. In the Second World War sixty million lost their lives and several million people were injured, besides the casualties that went unreported. America killed two hundred thousand civilians by dropping atom bombs on Hiroshima and Nagasaki, the number of the injured and those who turned homeless remaining unreported. The Russian Revolution caused the death of thirteen hundred thousand victims. In the Communist Revolution of China, the loss of life was somewhere between fourteen hundred thousand and twenty hundred thousand. Mussolini of Italy attacked the Muslim countries in Africa and put to death more than four hundred thousand Muslims, Stalin killed in the Civil War of Russia twenty million in which

---

distancing and the like are just preventive measures, not the cure for it. Whatever the reality, the USA, the only superpower of the world, is now the worst victim and is sending an SOS to China and India for help.

the majority of the victims were Muslims, and Hitler killed ten million people.[15]

When war was accepted as a natural way of settling disputes (under the garb of 'just war'), the party which had more sophisticated weapons had a better chance to win. This led to the production of weapons of mass destruction. It was then argued that only "civilized nations" could produce and sell them to less civilized nations with the restriction that they would not use it against their enemies "indiscreetly" and would not be the first to strike. This situation created a fear especially among non-nuclear nations and urged them to buy weapons from the nuclear nations, thus giving an impetus to arms trade which benefited only the nuclear superpowers. Arms trade soon emerged as the most profitable trade of the present time: weapons of mass destruction were bought at fabulously high price by even such nations which did not have enough to feed and educate their citizens. The result is that there is such a large number of such weapons in the world now that if, God-forbid, the situation goes out of control, our good earth could be destroyed several times by that lot.

The civilized nations justify arms trade by arguing that as countries in possession of nuclear weapons understand that if they behave irresponsibly, the world will meet swift and total destruction, leaving none to celebrate as victor. This

---

[15] Syed Hamid Mohsin, *Follow Me: Muhammad* (Bangalore: Salaam Centre, 2013), pp. 332-33.

realization, they argue, will work as a deterrent for all nuclear powers and force them to stick to their guns but never fire. Besides, it is said that as global trade has become so much important now to maintain a robust economy, all nations understand the importance of peaceful relationship with one another and will never take the risk of endangering it by opting for a war.[16] That is why, they claim, the world has not seen a war at a large scale in the recent past.

But this logic has failed to convince a good number of people. They argue that the idea of controlling war by producing weapons of mass destruction is bizarre. If the weapons so lethal and so expensive are bought and kept in stock as never-to be-used items, then why to produce them, improve them and buy and sell them when that money is so badly needed to fulfill basic needs of the citizens of the nations concerned? Who needs them any way and for what? And if no country needs them, why not ban their production?

There is yet another aspect to this issue. It is only a half-truth that by eliminating the possibility of traditional war we have made the world a haven of peace and security. The actual situation is that the "cyber war" will now replace "traditional war" and "atom bombs" will be replaced by "logic bombs." Now a well-informed and ill-intentioned techie can easily cause total disruption to the technological system of a target city, for example, and make the trains collide, airplanes

---

[16] Harari, *Homo Deus*, p. 17.

fly on routes never scheduled for them and make the people there think and behave in a way that he or she wants them to. The mind behind the game "Blue Whale" which prepared its players step by step to gladly commit suicide could do much more serious harm to humanity and at a much larger scale. And preparing viruses in the lab and releasing them into the borders of the enemy state, which may quickly spread all over the world and kill millions, is an apprehension that is in the air and is seriously challenging human imagination. And many more such threats could be added to the list.

Contribution of Western Civilization at the Intellectual Level

As mentioned earlier, the cognitive revolution has generated in humankind a tremendous ability to use mind: think, explore, experiment and discover. This has led humans to a new road to progress taking them to new heights of development. They have created space shuttles, conquered the moon, created stations in the space and are now exploring the possibility of establishing colonies on other planets. They have broken the atom and thus discovered the possibility of enormous amount of energy to be used for future projects. They have revolutionized communication system and with computer technology stepped into an arena of immense possibilities for further explorations.

Humans have now controlled time as well as space to a remarkable extent. Now they can finish a job in hours that required weeks and months in the past and connect to persons in a distant land by using a simple cell phone. They could chat with them by seeing them on the screen, send emails and voice messages, retrieve any information in minutes without moving from their armchair, and do the transaction of millions without touching a bill, to give only a few obvious examples.

With the help of science and technology, humans know and understand their physiological mechanism so much better now and are in a position to solve any problems at this level. Technological devices help them to find out with precision what disease, for example, is developing in their bodies and at what stage. They then can be sure that that disease can be treated by medicine, or surgery if medicine is not a good choice. By using surgery, they can repair the damage in their bodies even in most intricate areas. They can bypass blocked arteries, replace a damaged lever with a healthy lever donated by another person, and replace any sick organ with a donated healthy organ. If human organs are not available to help a patient, artificial organs prepared by science and technology can be used to give life support to him or her. By the way, such replacement of organs are routine practice now-a-days.

Or a Nano chip can be placed in a human body and connected to a computer program which could detect the formation of a disease in the human body and cure it at the right time as well. Atul Jalan writes; "Nanobots released into our blood streams can clean our blood streams and repair organs damaged by age or trauma."[17] In fact, all diseases could be thus controlled and all physical disabilities could be treated. Progress in medical science assures us now that humans could enjoy "perfect health."

This leads us to an interesting situation. If humans could fully overcome diseases which previously killed them, they can then hope to live longer. In fact, this has already been achieved. In the 20th century the average life span of humans has doubled from 40 to 70 years. When that has been done, it is also possible that in the 21st century their average life span will double again extending from 70 to 150 years.[18] While some scientists are skeptical about it, others believe that it has already become a fact of life. Jalan writes on the back of the cover of his book *Where Will Man Take Us?*: "The first man who will live for 150 years is already born."[19]

Again, if the target of 150 years is achieved, can man not further extend his life span? Scientists respond to this question with a confident 'yes.' They say that in view of scientific developments we can now safely talk about human life span as 500 years.[20]

---

[17] Jalan, p. 267.
[18] Harari, *Homo Deus*, p.29.
[19] Jalan, Back page of the cover of *Where Will Man Take Us?*.
[20] Harari, *Homo Deus,* p. 30.

And if life span can be extended that far, why not farther? Science and technology claim that by protecting human body from the ravages of disease and ageing and keeping it fully healthy and strong, humans will in future be able to defy death: they will enjoy "immortality."[21] Jalan says: "The prospect is staggering. A few tweaks to our DNA, to our hormonal systems, to our brain structures and we would be a superior, engineered race - free from disease and with a longer shelf life. Or even immortality."[22]

The attainment of immortality may raise some questions. What will happen to these immortal beings when they become old and infirm? Science says that it will fully control human ageing and infirmity. No matter what their age, humans will remain "ever young" and "perfectly healthy." By using Nano technology necessary changes can be made in a person's DNA which can transform an old and weak person into a strong young individual overnight. Jalan says that "they [nanobots] could soon even restore our DNA to how it was when we were in our twenties. This can turn fragile senior citizens into healthy young individuals overnight."[23]

But what about the boredom and monotony that longevity and immortality will bring to the life of humans? Again, science brushes aside this apprehension as baseless. It clarifies

---

[21] Harari, *Homo Deus*, p. 75.
[22] Jalan, p. 267.
[23] Jalan, p. 268.

that as frustration is caused by the internal mechanism of brain, not by the outer environment, it can be controlled: a "happiness pill" in the morning will ensure that humans enjoy perfect happiness the whole day.[24] Thus humans will be able to live a life of "immortality, bliss and divinity."[25]

....

So far, we have talked only about how science and technology could benefit humans at the physical level. But they can also directly enhance the intellectual capacity of humans to an astonishing extent. This mind-boggling revolution can be performed at two levels: one, Artificial Intelligence (AI) can be connected to human intelligence, resulting in enormous increase in human intelligence, and two, human intelligence is fed into the machines of artificial intelligence, thus creating such machines that are thousand times faster and smarter than the human mind. Either way, the resultant increase in intelligence will be beyond imagination.

In order to understand the future prospect of union between human intelligence and artificial intelligence, we can remind ourselves that at this stage humans will be able to communicate with a computer without talking or typing; they

---

[24] Jalan, p. 209.
[25] Harari, *Homo Deus*, p. 75.

will do so just by means of thoughts. A Nano chip can be fixed in the human brain which can be connected to a computer program, making it possible for the person concerned to convey his or her thoughts by means of electric signals. This facility will transfer the thoughts of the person concerned to the computer through electric signals which it will decode and convey its feedback to the human mind which it will immediately comprehend. This will give a new power to human mind and a new direction to its work capacity.[26] Mentioning a specific program in progress, Jalan informs that when it is successfully completed, "it can make the blind see and the deaf hear. And it can help humans communicate without typing, speaking or moving."[27] It could be recalled that Stephen Hawking used this device, called 'brain-computer interface' which helped him overcome his serious physical limitations and perform so well at the intellectual level.[28]

And if the same technology is used to connect with a computer program not just one but multiple brains in such a way that they can share and exchange data with one another, then what will happen? Then all the individual brains connected through a computer program will take data from one another and store them in their minds without having to read or listen to them. Each of them will be able to use the shared data as his or her own. Thus, by connecting an

---

[26] Harari, *Sapiens,* p. 456.
[27] Jalan, p. 271.
[28] Jalan, 270.

individual brain to multiple brains in the computer, the enormous increase in the intelligence of that individual will set new heights that we cannot imagine at this stage.[29]

If we take a look at the option of inventing a machine with human intelligence, we find that we are already using it in different forms in our daily life. Google Assistant and Google Map are ready examples of it which are just preliminary specimens of Artificial Intelligence (AI), referred to as Artificial Narrow Intelligence (ANI). The second stage of Artificial Intelligence is called Artificial General Intelligence (AGI). And the final stage which is most advanced so far, is known as Artificial Super Intelligence (ASI). For our discussion we will refer to Artificial Super Intelligence.

Now it is possible to create a human on computer which will have a complete human personality, like a normal human being with unique characteristics – individual emotions, thinking, hopes, aspirations, scruples and reservations. The only difference between this computer human and a real human will be that the computer human created by artificial intelligence will not have any physical existence outside the computer.

In fact, artificial intelligence could do better than just create a human on the computer. It can create a living being by using the DNA of a creature which will be one hundred percent like its source. This process is called cloning. Dolly, a lamb, was

---

[29] Harari, *Sapiens,* p. 456.

successfully created by cloning. This breakthrough has also made it possible to produce hybrid generations by using animals of two species, several of which are displayed at YouTube. The extinct specimens of birds and beasts can also be revived now by implanting their DNA in the womb of other suitable animals. A project to revive Dinosaur, an extinct species, is now under consideration by implanting its DNA in the womb of an elephant. Similarly, the species of Neanderthals that exists no more in the world can be recreated by placing their DNA in a woman's womb.

This brings science to yet another height of achievement. The power to recreate a dead species adorns science with the title of "creator:" if it could create, it is then god. And if it can play god, it has all the right to replace traditional religion. We, however, need to acknowledge here that as science could create a being only by using the DNA of a source creature that was already in existence, its creative power is restricted. Moreover, this cloned creature will be an exact replica of its DNA-providing source. This would establish that the power of science to create is very limited in comparison to that of the Supreme Being who had created the original source creature for the first time.

But science has overcome even this limitation. It is no more restricted to using the DNA of a creature as it is; it can change the DNA by rewriting it and thus create a being as it wants. *The Economist News Letter* reports: "Now genes can be written from scratch and edited repeatedly like text in a Word

Process." It is further mentioned in the same article that the advancement in synthetic biology has enabled scientists to rewrite the DNA of a human and design and create a human whose body may be as strong as a gorilla's and whose mind may never suffer any unhappiness or frustration.[30] Jalan also mentions that gene-editing is now within the access of science. He says, "Thanks to precision gene-editing techniques like CRISPR-Cas9, it won't be long before gene-editing is a regular feature that can be used to prevent most inheritable diseases. Why roll genetic dice when we know that intervention can ensure a healthy child."[31]

Thus, humans have freed themselves from slow evolutionary process caused by natural selection, and by means of cognitive revolution can now create desired changes in them which are fast, planned and controlled. The ability to do so is known as Intelligent Design (ID). Recently a French company created a florescent green rabbit on order: it planted the gene of a florescent green jelly fish in the embryo of a white rabbit. The baby thus born was a green rabbit. Its master called it Alba.[32] Alba was created by intelligent design, not by natural selection.

With the help of intelligent design, therefore, science can now bring unimaginable revolution in the form of life on earth.

---

[30] *The Indian Express,* Monday, April 8, 2019, p. 15.
[31] Jalan, p. 267.
[32] Harari, *Sapiens,* p. 447.

If it is not doing it at a large scale, it is not due to its lack of ability but owing to the moral questions involved. But can moral qualm and scruple stop this revolution? We should not forget that science and technology will fulfill immediate human needs as well. If the scientists find out a medicine which cures Alzheimer's (in which a human forgets a thing immediately) and protects and increases memory, can a human society stop science from developing a medicine along the same line which increases the memory of a normal human, say, five to ten times more?

So, when moralists will slowly lose ground and artificial intelligence will have a free hand, what will happen? Then, as Harari comments, "Humans will change beyond recognition."[33] Can we predict some of the changes? Let us try?

It is theoretically possible now that the 'intellectual self' of a human is separated from his or her "physical self," stored in a computer and saved on the cloud. This will emancipate human intelligence from the confines of physical self. If it is done and a society consisting of human intelligence entities thus comes into existence, can we call it a human society? Who will guide and control these human intelligence entities? Will their creators have control over them? And what kind of relationship will exist between human intelligence entities and the humans they were a part of? Let us see.

---

[33] Harari, *Homo Deus*, p. 16.

The fact is that if a computer program is designed by artificial super intelligence (ASI), it has a power to grow by itself and can go out of the control of its creator. Once created and let loose, it becomes fully independent and functions on its own. It evolves and increases its power by automatically learning from its experience. When the Russian chess world champion Garry Kasparov played against the Deep Blue computer program developed by IBM in 1996, he defeated Deep Blue, but in 1997 he lost against it simply due to the fact that the Deep Blue had learned from its mistakes and automatically improved its competence.[34] Harari acknowledges this fact in these words:

> Moreover, with the rise of machine learning and artificial neural networks, more and more algorithms evolve independently, improving themselves and learning from their own mistakes…. The seed algorithm may initially be developed by humans, but as it grows it follows its own path, going where no human has gone before – and where no human can follow.[35]

This gives birth to a horrifying apprehension about the possibility of machines taking over and enslaving humans. Stephen Hawking, the greatest physicist of our time, believed

---

[34] Jalan, pp. 23-25.
[35] Harari, *Homo Deus*, p. 458.

that it is a possibility.[36] And now that science has reached the stage of Quantum Computer, it is clear that humans are no match to machines that they will create. Jalan comments that the computing ability of quantum computers "would be equal to that of millions of conventional computers."[37]

This question can be looked at from a yet different angle. Is it also a possibility that instead of enslaving, *superhumans* simply decide to annihilate *Homo sapinens?* As the present generation of humans will after all be a misfit in the advanced superhuman civilization, this would be, according to the theory of evolution, a natural course of action. Commenting on the situation, Harari first acknowledges that "there seems to be no insurmountable technical barrier preventing us from producing superhumans"[38] and then predicts that the emergence of *superhumans* would bring a post-human era in which the master of the situation will be *superhumans*. If competition is a biological truth, *superhumans* will come into clash with *Homo sapience*, and if survival of the fittest is the law of nature, *superhumans* will prevail. Then, as Harari remarks, *superhumans* "would very likely bring down the curtain on Homo sapiens."[39]

---

[36] *The Indian Express,* "Stephen Hawking had warned against 'superhumans," Monday, 15 October 2018, p. 9.

[37] Jalan, p. 41.

[38] Harari, Sapiens, p. 453.

[39] Harari, *Sapiens*, p. 453.

Position of Western Civilization on Morality

The evolution theory disapproves that a moral code should be imposed on humans in the name of religion and culture. The Western society based on the ideals of evolution will allow full freedom to individuals so long as they do not bother others by their behavior. It will redefine morality by declaring that whatever is practically achievable and provides enjoyment to an individual or a group is moral, no matter how revolutionary it appears to be. The main thing is that individuals enjoy full freedom and the society functions smoothly with law and order system intact. The traditional moral code will gradually become redundant.

This is but natural that evolutionists do not subscribe to "morality" because morality teaches an individual to yield and honor the prescribed right-wrong paradigm set by age-old traditions while the theory of evolution is based upon the concept of stark competition. Will and Ariel Durant write:

So, the first lesson of history is that life is competition. Competition is not only the life of trade, it is the trade of life …. Co-operation is real, and increases with social development, but mostly because it is a tool and form of competition…. War is a nation's way of eating. It promotes co-operation because it is the ultimate form of competition.

According to the law of evolution humans do not have to be moral and nice to others; they have to be stronger and superior so as to be able to dominate others. Will and Ariel Durant explain this point in the following words:

> The second biological lesson of history is that life is selection.... Nature loves difference as the necessary material of selection and evolution; .... Inequality is not only natural and inborn, it grows with the complexity of civilization.... Freedom and equality are sworn and everlasting enemies, and when one prevails the other dies.[40]

Evolutionists argue that the moral teachings of the church have no scientific basis. Accordingly, Western civilization promotes in place of prescribed morality the concept of natural freedom, which means, as mentioned earlier, freedom to do anything which is practicable and imparts pleasure to the person or persons concerned. If, for example, two men or two women wish to live together as wife and husband and if it is practically possible for them to do so, it is, according to evolutionists, perfectly alright and natural and in the final stage, moral. Many countries, under the influence of Western civilization, have therefore accepted homosexual relationship as legal, passed laws in favor of it and proudly announce their support to it. Yuval Noah Harari, a male, dedicates his famous book *Lessons for the 21st Century* to his husband Itzik, along

---

[40] Will and Durant, pp. 19-20.

with others, and Prince William of England, as news appeared in an issue of *the Indian Express* of Delhi in June, 2019, announced that if his children liked to practice homosexuality after growing up, he would support them.

Such 'morals' are supported on the basis of an individual's freedom: what is wrong if two persons, whatever their gender, willingly establish physical relationship and live together like a family? If it makes them happy and is practically possible, they surely have a right to do so.

However, there are some questions regarding such absolute freedom in choosing a sex partner that greatly baffles those who disagree with the evolutionists. What will the society do, they ask, if some persons use this freedom to justify sexual relationship between parents and children, or between siblings: between son and mother, father and daughter, brother and sister? If that is what makes them happy and is practically possible, why should not they be allowed to do so?

Then the moral code for the future Western society will be like this: anything that is practically possible and enjoyable is moral.

Western Civilization and Spirituality

Science does not accept the existence of a soul in humans and so it automatically rejects spirituality. Evolutionists argue that the concept of soul is a religious myth and that there is no truth in the claim that humans, unlike animals, possess a soul which is a divine gift of God marking them as God's best creation.

According to religionists spirituality is a highly refined sensibility which arises in humans due to the presence of a soul in them and helps humans to connect to their Lord. But when there is no such divine being, as argued by evolutionists, there is no need of spirituality. Science accepts the physical and mental faculties of humans because they could be scientifically tested and proved, but it is not ready to go beyond that. Spirituality is beyond the realm of scientific investigation and therefore science does not accept its existence.

THREE

FUTURE OF HUMANKIND UNDER ISLAM

As in the previous section we evaluated modern Western civilization on four scales - material, intellectual, moral and spiritual - we will evaluate Islam now on the same scales and try to determine what prospect of an ideal human future it offers.

Islam's Guidelines at the Material Level

In Islam the material world in which we are living and the spiritual afterlife that it envisions are not contradictory. Islam of course attaches great prominence to success in the afterlife, but it identifies this world as the arena where humans could perform to qualify for it. That is why the concept of a purposeful lifestyle in this world is closely knit with the success in the afterlife within the doctrinal structure of Islam. The Qur'an records the dialogue between God and the angels about the creation of man and informs us that God convinced and silenced the angels by asking them and Adam names of some objects which were presented in front of them. It is important to note that those objects were material entities which belonged to this world, not to the heavens (Qur`an, 2: 30-33). Maulana Taqi Usmani in the commentary of the verses in question writes: "The names of things here refer to names of things found in this world and their characteristics, and to different human feelings, such as hunger, thirst, health and ailment."[41] Thus Adam's knowledge of the material things in the world justified his superiority over the angels and Adam and his progeny were given the responsibility of managing the affairs of the world as God's vicegerent.

Islam fully acknowledges the importance of human physical self and material environment, natural and created. According to its teachings, humans do not have to renounce the world and deny the natural urge for the fulfillment of physical needs. In order to attain a high level of spiritual relationship with their Creator, Muslims do not have to lead a life of renunciation, self-mortification and celibacy, as some religions require. They are encouraged to lead a normal life, eat well and dress properly, marry and love, build a happy family, achieve high education, religious and secular, and adopt a professional career by which they could contribute to the upkeep and progress of their society. Islam forbids its followers, however, from adopting such practices which are harmful and injurious at the individual or social level. With this stipulation in mind, Muslims can fully enjoy this-worldly life in

---

[41] Muhammad Taqi Uthmani, *Tawzeehul Qur`an*, (Delhi: Faisal International, 2017), p. 50, footnote 29.

its purity and bliss. According to a Hadith, if God blesses a person with material affluence, it should reflect in his or her dress and appearance as well, for that would be a proper acknowledgement of God's bounty and an expression of gratitude to Him. Abu al-Ahwas quoted his father as saying: I visited the Prophet, blessings and peace be upon him, wearing a poor garment. He asked me: Have you any property? My father replied in the affirmative. The Prophet enquired: What kind is it? My father replied: Allah has given me camels, sheep, horses and slaves. The Prophet then said: When Allah has given you property, let the mark of Allah's favor and honor to you be seen in your appearance."[42]

In fact, according to Islam, physical self is a very important part of human personality because it is it that enables humans to lead a religious life. They pray, fast, perform Hajj, and earn by which they pay *Zakat* and help the poor with charity. It is to be remembered that these are obligatory religious duties that all Muslims are asked to perform. Similarly, all other activities of benevolence which humans perform by using their body are counted in Islam as virtuous deeds apt to be rewarded in the afterlife. That is why Islam instructs its followers to maintain good health, seek treatment in sickness, stay away from harmful things such as alcohol and drugs, and never stoop down to the level of committing suicide.

---

[42] Abu Dawood, Hadith No. 4063; also Musnad Ahmad, Hadith No. 15892.

Also, Islam entrusts its followers to protect natural environment as best as possible. It declares that as vicegerent of God it is in fact a religious obligation of humankind to be nature-friendly and exploit natural resources only in the way which are for the benefit of humankind. They have to initiate and espouse research-oriented development projects in agriculture, industry, medicine, and the like, but they cannot indulge in any project such as the development of weapons of mass destruction. Planting of trees, for example, is symbolically acknowledged as an act of benevolence: a person who plants a tree will be rewarded even for the fruit that the travelers pick up and birds and animals consume. The Prophet of Allah once instructed his companions that if a person is out to plant a tree and in the midst of this engagement learns that the Final Hour (*Qayamat*) has arrived, he or she should go ahead and complete the job if time permits.[43] That is why even in a war Muslims are asked not to fell fruit-bearing trees in the land of the enemies in order to subjugate them. It is owing to this characteristic attitude of Muslims that architectural monuments such as the Taj Mahal of Agra and Alhambra of Spain, scientific inventions like the sea compass and various surgical instruments, and institutions of public welfare like

---

[43] Anas ibn Malik reported that the Prophet, may Allah bless him and grant him peace, said, "If the Final Hour comes while you have a palm-cutting in your hand and it is possible to plant it before the Hour comes, you should plant it." *Musnad Ahmad*, Hadith No. 12902 and 12981 (two narrations). Imam Bukhari has also mentioned this Hadith in his *Al-Adab al-Mufrad*. Hadith No. 479.

libraries and universities have been the distinct features of Muslim civilization. This point will be further explored later in this book.

Islam's Guidelines at the Intellectual Level

It is generally believed that religions are based on superstitions, myths and unqualified assumptions which have little to offer at the intellectual level. Islam is a glaring exception to this general rule. It accepts the value of "reason" and allots a prominent position to it in its belief system. It is significant to note that one of the prominent criteria to determine the validity of an Islamic law is "reason": it is rejected if it defies reason. Islam also attaches great importance to acquiring knowledge and identifies it as a mark of an Islamic character. The very first revelation (*wahiy*) of Islam began with the word "read," mentioned "learning by pen" and introduced the "formation of a human embryo from a clot of blood," which were the topics from the field of sophisticated learning and science, although this revelation descended upon an unlettered Arab who knew little about such things and was raised in a city in which only 17 persons could barely read and write. These verses are as follows:

Read! In the name of your Lord Who created
Created man from clots of blood

Read! And your Lord is the Most Bounteous
Who has taught the use of the pen,
Has taught man what he did not know. (Qur`an, 96: 1-5)

Other verses later revealed in the Qur`an invite its adherents to look around inquisitively, seek in nature signs of God's power as supreme creator and reflect on natural laws that so systematically operate to keep a miraculous equilibrium in the universe. Islam invites them repeatedly to "reflect," which is the first principle of science. In the Qur`an there is a long dialogue of Prophet Ibrahim (Abraham) who wanted to know how humans would be raised again on the Day of Judgment when so much time would have elapsed turning their bodies to dust. When God asked him if he did not believe in resurrection, he replied that he did, but his mind was unable to comprehend how the particles would be recollected and joined together to recreate the former bodies exactly in the same form. It was a rational question, but God did not mind. Instead, He satisfied him by providing an evidence at the rational level (Qur`an, 2: 260). It only shows that although in Islam rationality and revelation (*wahiy*) operate at different levels, they unite at a higher level to form a belief code which provides a profound rational basis to support Prophet Ibrahim's spiritual experience.

With the first revelation of Islam a new era of enlightenment began. No wonder that Islam designates the pre-Islamic period as the era of *Jahiliya*, i. e. the period of ignorance, and the severest opponent of the Prophet at

Makkah was nicknamed as Abu Jahl, the "father or epitome of ignorance."

Thus, in trying to comprehend the material world and phenomena of nature with the help of reason and intellect, Islam is fully compatible with science. Western writers of our time recognize this fact and acknowledge it in clear words. Maurice Bucaille, a contemporary scientist, says:

> . . . for Islam, religion and science have always been considered twin sisters. From the very beginning, Islam directed people to cultivate science; the application of this precept brought with it the prodigious strides in science taken during the great era of Islamic civilization, from which before the Renaissance the West itself benefited.[44]

A necessary clarification

At this point I would like to leave the discussion of the main topic here for a while and take the liberty to clarify a point which is important from the point of view of the main objective of this study. My standpoint in this study is that Islam is the direct source of the guidelines that are responsible for the growth of the Islamic civilization we are discussing in

---

[44] Maurice Bucaille, *The Bible, the Quran and Science* (Delhi: New Crescent, 2012), p. ix.

this book. All such guidelines are based on the teachings of the Qur`an and Hadith; in most cases even secondary details are provided. It is not the case that these guidelines are later added by Muslim scholars. For example, when Maurice Bucaille acknowledged scientific spirit of Islam, as mentioned in the above quotation, he did so on the basis of his direct reading of the Qur`an, not by following the suggestion of any Muslim scientist who appeared later and obliged the world with a revealing observation. This should also be noted that this is not the case with other religions, as some Western writers quoted later in this work clearly point out. It is important to take cognizance of the fact that Islamic scriptures are uniquely contemporary and relevant which can guide humankind to an ideal future in changing times.

Unfortunately, this point has sometimes been missed even by those Western scholars who are fully appreciative of the Muslim contributions in the field of science and technology. For example, Gustave Le Bon, whose work on Islamic civilization in French is a masterpiece, comments that the Qur`an did not have anything to contribute in the scientific progress that the Arabs/Muslims achieved. He writes:

> Throughout all the scientific and philosophical doctrines which the Arabs propagated in the world for more than five centuries, the influence of the Koran [Qur`an] was non-existent, just like the role of the Bible in modern scientific works. The Koran was a body of doctrines which men of learning respected to a greater and lesser

degree, because it was responsible for the power of the Arabs, and was well suited to the needs of the masses, who were in any case unable to benefit from the teachings of science and philosophy. Yet Arab scientists and men of learning were not unduly worried by the discrepancies between their discoveries and the theories of the sacred book.[45]

Le Bon has missed a vital point here and his thesis put above needs to be revised in the light of recent research. Modern scholars acknowledge that, unlike other scriptures, the Qur'an is scientific in spirit and content and its teachings are miraculously contemporary. The statements of some recent Western scholars quoted below will further substantiate this point.

....

Now we will resume the main discussion and refer back to the above quotation of Bucaille in which he calls Islam and science as twin sisters. It is important to note that in order to directly read the Qur'an with a view to check the status of information on science provided in it, Bucaille learned the Arabic language and studied the Qur'an directly. His

---

[45] Gustave Le Bon, *The World of Islamic Civilization,* translated from French into English by David Macrae (Spain: Tudor Publishing Company, 1974), p. 142.

comments on the Qur`an are thus based on his first-hand knowledge of it. He came to the following conclusion:

> I knew from translations that the Qur'an made allusion to all sorts of natural phenomena, but I had only a summary knowledge of it. It was only when I examined the text very closely in Arabic that I kept a list of them at the end of which I had to acknowledge the evidence in front of me: the Qur'an did not contain a single statement that was assailable from a modern scientific point of view.[46]

Maurice Bucaille acknowledges this surprising fact that certain scientific discoveries which are very recent, not older than hundred to hundred and fifty years, are clearly mentioned in the Qur`an which was revealed more than fourteen hundred years ago. The specific details that he provides could be checked in his book but we could read below his acknowledgment of this fact where he also comments that other scriptures are devoid of this quality. He says:

> . . . the Quran, while inviting us to cultivate science, itself contains many observations on natural phenomena and includes explanatory details which are seen to be in

---

[46] Bucaille, p. viii.

total agreement with modern scientific data. There is no equal to this in Judeo-Christian Revelation.[47]

Maurice Bucaille is not alone in acknowledging the scientific nature and spirit of Islam: there is a large number of renowned Western scholars who attest to it. Professor Emeritus Keith L. Moore, a scholar of international repute in anatomy and embryology and author of the much-celebrated book *The Developing Human*, said in the Seventh Medical Conference held in Dammam in 1981:

> It has been a great pleasure for me to help clarify statements in the Qur`an about human development. It is clear to me that these statements must have come to Muhammad from God, because almost all of this knowledge was not discovered until many centuries later. This proves to me that Muhammad must have been a messenger of God.

Keith Moore comments that a new system of classification of stages in the development of human embryo could be developed by using the terminology mentioned in the Qur'an and Sunnah (what Muhammad, peace be on him, said, did or approved of). He says:

> . . . although Aristotle, the founder of the science of embryology, realized that chick embryos developed in stages from his studies of hen's eggs in the fourth

---

[47] Bucaille, pp. 115-16.

century B. C., he did not give any details about these stages. As far as it is known from the history of embryology, little was known about the staging and classification of human embryos until the twentieth century. For this reason, the description of the human embryo in the Qur'an cannot be based on scientific knowledge in the seventh century.[48]

Dr. Alfred Kroner, a world-renowned geologist and a professor and Chairman of the Department of Geology at the Institute of Geosciences, Johannes Guttenberg University in Germany, was surprised to find a clear statement in the Qur`an about the common origins of the earth and the sun, the moon, the galaxies, etc. He has the following to say:

> I think it is almost impossible that he [Prophet Muhammad] could have known about things like the common origins of the universe, because scientists have only found out within the last few years, with very complicated and advanced technological methods, that this is the case.

He further says:

> Somebody who did not know something about nuclear physics fourteen hundred years ago could not, I think, be

---

[48] I. A. Ibrahim, *A Brief Illustrated Guide to Understanding Islam*, Houston, Darussalam, 1997, pp. 10-11.

in a position to find out from his own mind, for instance, that the earth and the heavens have the same origin.[49]

Dr. T. V. N. Persaud, Professor of Anatomy, Pediatrics and Child Health, and Professor of Obstetrics, Gynecology and Reproductive Sciences at the University of Manitoba in Canada, makes a revealing comment about the accurate scientific knowledge conveyed to humanity fourteen hundred years ago in the Qur`an:

> The way it was explained to me is that Muhammad was a very ordinary man. He could not read, didn't know [how] to write. In fact, he was an illiterate. And we're talking about twelve [actually about fourteen] hundred years ago. You have someone illiterate making profound pronouncements and statements and that are amazingly accurate about scientific nature. And I personally can't see how this could be a mere chance. There are too many accuracies and, like Dr. Moore, I have no difficulty in my mind that this is a divine inspiration or revelation which led him to these statements.[50]

Dr. Joe Leigh Simpson, a specialist of Obstetrics and Gynecology from America, especially refers to two sayings of

---

[49] Ibrahim, pp. 16-17.

[50] Ibrahim, pp. 27-28. Dr. Persaud has cited some Qur`anic verses and hadith (Traditions of the Prophet Muhammad) in some of his books and lectures.

Prophet Muhammad (hadith)[51] and after confirming the authenticity of information conveyed in them, recommends that science can take help from Islamic sources (Qur`an and Hadith) in its pursuit of knowledge. He says:

> . . . these hadeeths could not have been obtained on the basis of the scientific knowledge that was available [at] the time of their writing .... It follows, I think, that not only there is no conflict between genetics and religion but, in fact, religion [he means Islam here] can guide science by adding revelation to some of the traditional scientific approaches, that there exist statements in the Qur`an shown centuries later to be valid, which support knowledge in the Qur`an having been derived from God.[52]

Dr. William W. Hay, a well-known marine scientist and a professor of geological sciences at the University of Colorado, USA, was presented with some verses from the Qur`an that deal with the sea and the ocean. After studying them, he was truly surprised to notice that the information in them was not only authentic; it was also recent, certainly not known at the

---

[51] These prophetic traditions (*Hadith*) are as follows: (1) "In every one of you, all components of your creation are collected together in your mother's womb by forty days," *Muslim and Bukhari,* Nos. 2643 and 3208, respectively. (2) "When forty-two nights have passed over the embryo, God sends an angel to it who shapes it and creates its hearing, vision, skin, flesh and bones...." Muslim, No. 2645.

[52] Ibrahim, pp. 28-29.

time of the revelation of the Qur`an. He had the following to say:

> "I find it very interesting that this sort of information is in the ancient scriptures of the Holy Qur`an, and I have no way of knowing where they would come from, but I think it is extremely interesting that they are there ...."
> He concluded by saying: "Well, I would think it must be the divine being."[53]

Dr. Yoshihide Kozai, Professor Emeritus at Tokyo University and former Director of the National Astronomical Observatory, Mitaka, Japan, comments on the astronomical information provided in the Qur`an in these words:

> I am very much impressed by finding the astronomical facts in [the] Qur`an .... So, by reading [the] Qur`an and by answering to the questions, I think I can find my future way for investigation of the universe.[54]

These are only a few names that we have mentioned here as examples. In fact, the list is long enough and cannot be accommodated in this short book. These themes are covered in short articles as well as full-length books which are available on *amazon.com*; some of them are also cited in the bibliography of this study. There are also helpful websites

---

[53] Ibrahim, pp. 29-30.
[54] Ibrahim, p. 30.

providing information on this topic, such as *www.islam-guide.com/science*. *A Brief Illustrated Guide to Understanding Islam* also provides names and addresses of some organizations on its pages 69-70 that can help those who wish to seek further information on the above topic.

....

We discussed above how Islam is different from other religions in its scientific nature and in its ability to lead and give a new direction to scientific pursuits. It has no conflict with science in its interpretation of the physical world and has contributed to the scientific progress and civilizational growth of humankind in the recent past. When Muslims had to fight the Romans, they came across the works of the Greek scholars which the Romans were unable to appreciate due to their different cultural inclination and preference. The Muslims protected those works, brought them to their capital and got them translated into Arabic by spending significant amount of time, money and energy over them. The Caliph Mamun Rashid used to give the translator gold equal the weight of the book that he translated. It is significant to note that those works of the Greek scholars were not related to Islam, the Arabic language or the Arab culture. The Muslims went out of way to protect them only because Islam had taught them that knowledge is a single entity including the secular and the religious and that it has to be respected in its own right. If a piece of knowledge is useful for humankind, Muslims will try to benefit from it, no matter where they find it, but if it is harmful, it will be proved so and discarded. As the prophet of Islam had taught them: Knowledge is the lost property of Muslims; wherever they find it, they will strive their best to acquire it.[55]

For the translation of the Greek masterpieces, Haroon Rashid, the then caliph of Muslims, established in his capital an academic center called *Darul Hikmah*, which is translated as *the House of Science* by Robert Briffault in his famous book *The Making of Humanity*. Masterpieces of Greek thinkers, Plato, Aristotle, Galen, Ptolemy, and others, were translated into Arabic from this very institution. These translations later became a source of information about the philosophies of the Greeks for the Europeans in the post-Renaissance period. Robert Briffault writes:

> It is highly probable that but for the Arabs [read 'Muslims'] modern European civilization would never have arisen at all; it is absolutely certain that for them, it would not have assumed that character which has enabled it to travel all previous phases of evolution. For although there is not a single aspect of European growth in which the decisive influence of Islamic culture is not traceable, nowhere is it so clear and momentous as in

---

[55] It was narrated by Abu Huraira that the Messenger of Allah said, "A word of wisdom is the lost property of the believer. Wherever he finds it he has more right to acquire it." *(Sunan Ibn Maaja,* Hadith No. 4169)

the genesis of that power which constitutes the paramount distinctive force of the modern world and the supreme source of its victory – natural science and the scientific spirit. [56]

Phillip K. Hitti also appreciates the contribution of the Arabs by acknowledging the value of the translations by which the Muslims saved Greek knowledge from being lost. Many of the original Greek works are in fact lost forever; they are now available to the world only in Arabic translations from which they were later translated in European languages. And transmission, from the standpoint of the history of culture, is no less essential than origination, for had the researches of Aristotle, Galen and Ptolemy been lost to posterity the world would have been as poor as if they had never been produced. The line of demarcation between translated and original work is, of course, not always clearly drawn. Many of the translators were also contributors.[57]

While translating the Greek masterpieces, the Muslim scholars also made important additions to the knowledge that those books contained. Hitti writes that Europe owes to the Muslims the knowledge on which it built its educational policies later on.

---

[56] Briffault, Robert, *The Making of Humanity*, London: George Allen & Urwin, 1919, p. 190.

[57] Philip K. Hitti, *The Arabs: A Short History* (Washington D.C.: Regnery Publishing, 1996), p. 141.

By now the Arabs had not only assimilated the ancient lore of Persia and the classical heritage of Greece, but had adapted both to their own peculiar needs and ways of thinking. Their translations, modified by the Arab mind in the course of several centuries, were passed on, together with many new contributions, to Europe through Syria, Spain and Sicily and laid the basis of that canon of knowledge which dominated medieval European thought.[58]

Muslims took knowledge to new heights in yet another way. They made Greek philosophy a science by introducing Inductive logic and experimental method and spread scientific knowledge through their academic writings and universities. Le Bon provides abundant evidence in his book to support each of these claims. He writes:

> The experimental method begun by them was certain to lead them to major discoveries. As we shall see, they crammed more scientific discoveries into three or four centuries than the Greeks had managed to attain in a much longer time. But the Arabs did more than make scientific discoveries: they disseminated them far and wide, through their books and universities, with a particularly great impact on Europe.[59]

---

[58] Hitti, p. 141.
[59] Le Bon, p. 36.

Le Bon further comments:

> Experiment and observation were the method of the Arabs. Book learning and repetition of the master's opinion was that of medieval Europe. This difference is fundamental to any understanding of the scientific merits of the Arabs.[60]

It was Muslims who introduced the experimental method of investigation to the world which made the emergence of science possible. What we call science today came into existence by virtue of new methods of investigation which were unknown to the Greeks. Briffault writes:

> The debt of our science to that of the Arabs does not consist in startling discoveries or revolutionary theories; science owes a great deal more to Arab culture, it owes its existence. The ancient world was, as we saw, pre-scientific.[61]

The Muslims also developed the Arabic language into a language of science and technology and produced original writings in it which made valuable additions in different fields of knowledge. Montgomery Watt writes:

> ... [A]t least under the Umayyads the Arabs themselves achieved much. It is even more important, however, to notice that the clients who took part in the early

---

[60] Le Bon, p. 35.
[61] Briffault, p. 191.

intellectual movement had, as far as we can tell, become Arabized in that they had accepted and become bearers of the Arab ethos. One mark of this is their enthusiasm for the Arabic language. Even if not all the writers were Arabs, it was mainly Arab influences which were moulding the new intellectual culture.[62]

Watt further clarifies: "In the period from 800 to 1300 medical writings in Arabic have been preserved from the pens of over seventy authors, mostly Muslims, but including a few Christians and Jews."[63] These works served as textbooks in Western universities for centuries.

There is a very long list of Muslim scientists, scholars and practitioners who contributed to the growth of knowledge in almost every important field much earlier than the Renaissance in Europe and were in fact the pioneers. To cover their contributions in this short book will be too ambitious. Zakariya Razi (Razes), Ibn Sina (Avicenna), Jabir bin Hayyan, Al-Khwarizmi, Al-Kindi, Omar Khayyam, Ibn Rushd and Ibn Khaldun are only a few names to cite here, each of whom deserves a book-length study; others who are equally important, cannot even be mentioned here just by their names.[64] Instead of attempting a sketchy description of them

---

[62] Watt, p. p. 88.

[63] Watt, p. 227.

[64] I have mentioned a few of them in my book *Islam: Architect of a Progressive Civilization,* which is available on *amazon.com* and *kindle* under my name. The bibliography of this book also contains titles of some books

here which would in fact be a disservice to them, I refer the readers to the relevant books which deal with the topic in detail. I however quote below a passage from a famous historian Dr. Tara Chand to establish how wide and deep the contributions of Muslims were in the field of science:

> For a thousand years this civilization [Muslim civilization] was the central light whose rays illumined the world. It was the mother of European culture, for men reared in this civilization were the masters in the Middle Ages at whose feet the Spaniards, the French, the English, the Italians and the Germans sat to learn philosophy, sciences of mathematics, astronomy, chemistry, physics, medicine and industrial techniques. Their names are household words.[65]

Thus, we can see that Islam has a very rich legacy in science which qualifies it as a strong protagonist of scientific progress contesting Western civilization at the intellectual level.

---

that deal with this topic. Many more references could be traced on the internet.

[65] Tara Chand, Presidential Address, Fourth All India Islamic Studies Conference, 25-27 December, 1964, Osmania University, Hyderabad, p. 23, quoted by Ziauddin Ahmad, p. xx.

Islamic Guidelines at the Moral Level

As Islam is a religion, it attaches much importance to morality and offers a clear, complete and exhaustive blue print of its moral teachings for all spheres of life. It holds that when a society comes into existence, it will naturally consist of men and women, young and old, rich and poor, black and white, weak and strong, and unless their rights and duties are clearly defined and fully supported by moral laws, there will be chaos instead of peace and confrontation instead of cooperation. That is why Islam connects its moral code with its religious teachings and directs Muslims to fulfill their moral responsibilities with sincere God-consciousness. And that is why the Prophet of Islam is reported to have said, "I've been sent to the world as a Messenger for perfecting the moral code of conduct" (*Musnad Ahmad*, Hadith No. 8952). The moral injunctions of Islam encompass the whole of human life, a very brief sketch of which is presented below.

At the 'individual' level, Islam teaches that each Muslim should uphold the best possible moral conduct in personal life, eschew all moral irregularities and lead a life of uprightness. The Qur'an declares that the noblest among humans in God's sight is the one who is the most pious. (Qur'an 49: 13)

At the 'family' level, Islam encourages Muslims, men and women, to extend their personal moral benevolence to a larger level by observing cordial relationship with other members of the family. After defining mutual rights and duties of each member in the family, Islam emphasizes that Muslims should try to be duty-oriented instead of being right-conscious; they should be broad-minded enough even to forego their rights over others just to avoid clash and conflict in the family. It could be imagined that its immediate gain will be a peaceful home and family and the ultimate reward, which is in the hands of God, will be much sweeter.

At the 'neighborhood' level, Islam instructs Muslims to establish a cordial and duty-oriented relationship with neighbors, no matter whether they are Muslims or non-Muslims, good neighbors or trouble makers, residents of their immediate neighborhood or temporary companions at work places, or co-travelers who share space with them temporarily.

At the 'social' level, Islam exhorts that Muslims should fully cooperate with one another in establishing in the society what is good and never side with anybody in doing anything bad and harmful in the society: "Help one another in goodness and in piety. Do not help one another in sin and transgression" (Qur`an 5: 2). Virtue and justice will be upheld by Muslims all the time and at all levels in the name of Islam even if they have to refuse to help a co-believer and side with a follower of another faith. The prophet instructed his followers to stop a Muslim from doing an injustice (a tyrannical act) and considered it a help to him that he deserved as a co-believer. (Bukhari, Hadith No. 6952). In addition, a Muslim is instructed to share his wealth with the disadvantaged Muslims by giving them 2.5 per cent of his savings annually which is called *Zakah* and is one of the five fundamental pillars of Islam. This is an obligatory duty for Muslims and is in addition to the philanthropic charities that they are encouraged to give to any deserving person, regardless of his or her religious association.

Concerning Muslims' moral and social duties to 'non-Muslims,' Islam instructs its adherents to relate to them cordially at the social level and participate in their grief and happiness. Once when a bier was passing within the sight of the Prophet of Islam, he immediately rose from his seat to show respect for the departed soul. When his companions informed him that the bier was that of a Jew, not of a Muslim, he replied, "Was he not a human being?" (Muslim, Hadith No. 961). According to the teachings of Islam, non-Muslims will be accommodated respectfully at all levels in the Muslim society and state, to which the treaties signed by the Prophet and the Caliphs bear witness. A non-Muslim girl from the background of *Ahlal Kitaab* (Jews and Christians who believe in one God) can Islamically marry a Muslim man and, if she does not like to convert to Islam, follow her own religion with full freedom and dignity in her Muslim husband's house. By the way, this provision is not granted in Christianity or Judaism.[66] Khalid Saifullah Rahmani, an eminent Islamic jurist, brings out a subtle point symbolizing Islamic benevolence and says: "In

---

[66] This topic has been dealt with in some detail in my book, *Is Islam a Violent Religion* (available on *amazon.com* and also on *kindle* under my name).

spite of the religious differences, Muslims can pledge a property as *waqf* (endowment) in the name of a non-Muslim individual, or even a non-Muslim religious institution, such as a church."[67] In the historic event of the conquest of Makkah, the Prophet gave the key of the *Baitullah*, the Holy Al-Haram, to 'Uthman bin Talha Sheybi who was a polytheist then and made him the custodian of the holiest Islamic shrine on earth; Sheybi accepted Islam later.[68] Islam announces in clear terms its message, invites all to consider it and accept it by their free choice, but in honoring their right to decline and in granting those who decline a right to remain a respectable part of the Muslim society, it sets an example.

At the 'human' level, Islam identifies its audience as humans, not Arabs. The Qur'an addresses its readers from the beginning to the end by the words, "O humans (*ya ayyuhan naas*)," never on the tribal or racial basis as the Quraysh or the Arabs. When the Prophet began preaching in Makkah, his call to Makkans was, "*O humans, say that there is no deity worthy of worship except the one God Allah, you will achieve true prosperity*" (*ya ayyuhan naas, qulu la ilaha illallah wa tuflihu*)." In the Qur'an God introduced Himself as the "Cherisher of mankind," not of the Arabs (*Rabbin naas*), and, according to a Hadith, He calls all human beings as His family and announces

---

[67] Khalid Saifullh Rahmani, *Inquilab*, the Urdu daily, Delhi edition, Monday, August 29, 2016.

[68] Sayyid Suleiman Nadwi, *Seeratun Nabi*, vol. 6 (Azam garh: Darul Musannifin, 2011), p. 271.

that the person who is most caring to humans is the best in His sight. (*Mo'jam Al Kabeer,* Tabrani: Hadith No. 10/86).

Islam clearly protects the rights of 'animals' and exhorts Muslims to be kind to them in all respects. It holds humans responsible for properly feeding the animals that they keep, not take extra services from them and never treat them cruelly. It permits humans to sacrifice animals for procuring food, but it forbids them from killing an animal for sport, or from burning insects like ants to get rid of them, or separating chicks from the mom birds. It is an Islamic courtesy to provide food and drink to an animal which is going to be sacrificed the next moment. Muslims who are in *Ihraam* for performing Hajj are instructed by the Islamic *Shariah* not to kill an animal, a bird or an insect (in the same way that they are asked not to commit a sin); if they do any such thing, their Hajj will not be accepted unless they pay the prescribed compensation for it.

As far as 'nature' is concerned, Muslims have to be fully mindful of safeguarding natural environment and are responsible not to cause any damage to it. Muslims do not worship nature, but they cannot cause any harm to it by disturbing its environmental equilibrium. As mentioned earlier, even in a war situation, a Muslim army attacking a city cannot fell trees bearing fruit or burn the crops standing in the field to subjugate an enemy. Also, Muslims performing Hajj are religiously forbidden from plucking a branch of a tree, or a leaf, or even a naturally grown blade of grass; if he does so, he will have to pay a penalty in order for his Hajj to be acceptable.

Islam prefers peace to war in all situations. It teaches in clear words that "peace is better and preferable" (Qur`an, 4:128), but if a war breaks out, it recommends all possible moral restraints and humanitarian concessions to the opponent to save them from its harm. For example, a Muslim army in action has to restrain itself from attacking, killing or harassing a woman, a minor, an old person, a handicapped, or civilians who stay indoors and do not participate in war. The Muslims are instructed not to fight soldiers of the enemy if they seek peace, or lay down their arms to signal that they do not wish to fight, or run away from the battlefield implying that they are giving up: they will not be chased, arrested and punished. Islam teaches that if a soldier of the enemy falls injured in the battlefield, he will not be killed, but picked up for treatment. A medical squad intending to help the injured in the battlefield will not be attacked, a messenger for peace talk will never be killed and a massacre will never be allowed after a victory.[69]

---

[69] For details, see my book Is Islam a violent Religion? on amazon.com and kindle.

Islamic Teachings at the Spiritual Level

Unlike the evolutionists and scientists, Islam endorses the spiritual status of humans. It acknowledges that a "soul" is an essential part of a human self and is a divine gift (*amr Rabb*) distinguishing humans from animals. It teaches that it is the soul in humans that creates in them a sensibility called spirituality which is the highest in the hierarchy of the four faculties that we mentioned before. It is the soul that engenders in humans a natural urge to seek and connect to their Creator and produces in them an in-built liking for virtues and a disgust for wickedness. By virtue of spirituality humans develop cleanliness of heart and piety of character and build a society in which all relate to one another benevolently because their Lord has commanded so. The stage of spirituality is higher than that of morality: in morality, a human relates to other humans, but by spirituality he or she rises higher to God and becomes a part of the entire scheme of creation.

As spirituality helps humans to live in peace with their Creator, it also makes it possible for them to live in peace with other humans, in fact the whole creation. Spirituality liberates humans from unnecessary frustration and conflict; by connecting to the Lord of the world they find contentment even when goings are rough. It prepares them to enjoy life at the physical level, employ their rational ability for the good of the society, support togetherness by following moral values, and find all this spiritually rewarding because they are doing that for their Lord.

It is at the stage of spirituality that Islam's distinction in comparison to science is most evident. Islam endorses 'messengership,' 'revelation' (*wahiy*) and 'afterlife' which are the spiritual sources of divine guidance. Science of course does not recognize *messengership*, *revelation* and *afterlife* because they cannot be proved at the rational level: they cannot be proved at the rational level, says religion, not because they do not exist, but because they are higher stages of reality and need different faculties to perceive them. As the sensory faculties found in humans cannot fully discern reason, reason cannot fully comprehend soul. Imam Ghazali, an eminent Islamic scholar, says:

> There is nothing unreasonable in the assumption that, above the sphere of reason, there exists another sphere — that of divine revelation; while we are completely ignorant of the laws which govern it, it is enough for the reason to admit the possibility that it exists.[70]

It is to be noted that spirituality, which is inspired by revelation (*wahiy*), has a strong relevance to this mundane life and is in fact a this-worldly need. Reason is essential, which Islam acknowledges, but it alone is not able to guide humans to the discovery of the whole truth about the scheme of life. In

---

[70] Quoted in Le Bon, pp. 46-47.

Western civilization reason and spirituality are at odds, but in Islam they are compatible. It is irrational to believe that whatever is beyond the realm of scientific experimentation is necessarily non-existent. W. Montgomery Watt makes a relevant observation on this issue in the following words:

> The struggle or tension between Semitic intuition and Greek reason is one that has not been yet settled or resolved. We Westerners tend to admire Greek reason for we realize that it is the source of our amazing scientific achievements, though we are beginning to understand something of its limitations. We must certainly not despise Semitic intuition, since, in the form of revealed scriptures of Judaism and Islam, it has been the basis of some of the most stable communities the world has known.[71]

Thus, we see that Islamic teachings inspire all spheres of life: physical, intellectual, moral and spiritual. Islam does not consider any of these faculties as negative which has to be renounced in order to gain an access to a higher level of excellence. It teaches that these faculties are in fact divine gifts built into human nature and an ideal Islamic personality can come into existence only by forging them into a balanced synthesis. If humans succeed in achieving such a balanced personality, they will have no conflict, discontentment or a feeling of fragmentation. They will live a full and wholesome

---

[71] Watt, p. 255.

life and will create a wholesome environment around them. And when they will be about to depart from the world, they will experience the bliss of the divine promise: "O contented soul! Return to your Lord in the state that thou art pleased with Him and that He is pleased with you" (Qur`an, 89: 27-28).

FOUR

WESTERN CIVILIZATION VERSUS ISLAM
A SUMMARY

In the above sections we have discussed the question about the future of humankind and tried to investigate which of the two, Western civilization or Islam, guarantees its safety and glory better. We studied this question separately in the light of the promises and performances of modern Western civilization and of Islam separately at different levels. It is time now that we pinpoint the major differences between the two and see point by point what each of them is apt to offer.

1. Is there a creator of humans?

Evolutionists say that life was born on earth by virtue of certain natural laws which has evolved to the present form of *Homo sapiens* by passing through evolutionary stages in which no creator played any role. They argue that the concept of a creator is religion-based which is not acknowledged by science. Whatever is happening in the arena of life is, according to scientists, controlled by laws of nature and is tied up by the chain of cause-and-effect relations.

Islamists say that humans, as all else in the world, are 'created,' not evolved. The cause and effect chain that evolutionists talk about is of course there and is determined by certain laws of nature, but those laws themselves have been created and given an operational power by a superhuman being that Islam calls God. Islamists urge that the existence of natural laws that explain the systematic functioning of the mechanism of nature does not necessarily disprove that there is a creator and controller of those laws. Science rejects God because it is not able to relate to Him by physical senses and intellect and is not ready to perceive Him at the spiritual level; it denies God's existence because it does not know Him, not because it has proved that He does not exist. A scholar like Jean Jacques Rousseau also accepts the need of a supreme divine being that holds the central position in the scheme of life and gives it a meaning. He writes:

> To discover the rules of society that are best suited to nations, there would need to exist a superior existence who could understand the passions of men without feeling any of them, who had no affinity with our nature but knew it to the roots, whose happiness was independent of ours but who would nevertheless make

our happiness our concern. . . . In fact, a divine lawgiver is needed.[72]

2. Do humans have a purpose in life?

Science says that there is no purpose behind life. It asserts that as humans are not 'created' by God, they are not responsible to anybody for their behavior in any way and have no purpose in life to fulfill. Yuval Noah Harari says, "As far as we can tell, from a purely scientific viewpoint, human life has absolutely no meaning. Humans are the outcome of blind evolutionary processes that operate without goal or purpose."[73]

Islam says that humans have been created for the noble purpose to lead a life in accordance with God's injunctions and, as His vicegerent, to promote virtue and justice on earth and discourage evil and injustice (Qur'an, 3: 110). They are supposed to remain fully committed to this aim and strive to establish on earth an order that could guarantee peace and justice to all, irrespective of their sex, race, color, nationality or creed. They are also taught that if they comply with the divine will in fulfilling the objective of their creation, they should hope to be richly rewarded in the hereafter.

---

[72] Jean Jacques Rousseau, *Social Contract*, Book II, Chapter 6: "The Lawgiver," quoted by Sayyed Mujtaba Musavi Lari, *Western Civilization Through Muslim Eyes,* translated by F. J. Goulding (Qom: Foundation of Islamic C. P. W., 2008), p. 56.

[73] Harari, *Sapiens*, p. 438.

3. Do humans have a soul?

Scientists deny the existence of a soul in humans because they do not find it in a human body through scientific investigation. Harari comments: "There is zero scientific evidence that in contrast to pigs, Sapiens have souls."[74] It has to be understood that science does not accept the existence of a soul in humans because if it does, it will have to accept the role of God as creator Who did this special favor to humans. The evolution theory cannot subscribe to the idea that the presence of a soul in humans was a result of natural selection which all other species failed to achieve for reasons that science cannot establish.

Islam says that a soul is indeed a prominent part of human personality which is a special divine gift to humankind and justifies their qualification as God's vicegerent. It is the soul which exhorts humans to adopt moral excellence, relate to their Creator and consequently develop a high level of sensibility with which to build a special relationship with God. It is on the strength of their spiritual excellence that humans inculcate virtue and compassion in them with which to create a benevolent society, culture and civilization for mankind.

---

[74] Harari, *Homo Deus,* p. 119.

4. Are humans obliged to follow a moral code of conduct?

Science says that as there is no god, no afterlife and no Judgment Day, following a prescribed moral code is not an obligation for humans; in fact, morality has no meaning at all. If, for example, humans have an urge in them for the gratification of sexual desire, they could just do that in whatever way it suits them, for as long as it is an in-born urge, it is natural and, therefore, moral. They suggest that if there has to be a moral code for the society to function smoothly, it should be majority-friendly. Whatever the majority of a population likes and approves, it should be allowed in practice as moral. Homosexuality was considered immoral in the past civilizations because the majority looked at it as immoral, but it is moral now, duly protected by law in many countries, because the majority now approves of it. Incidentally, democracy is also based on the very idea of the legality of the sanction of the majority.

Islam says that morality forms an essential part of an individual's personality and is necessary for the integrity of the society. A society without moral foundations defies human nature and will not be able to provide justice to its members; all values will crumble down and all relationships will be thrown into disarray. That is why Islam offers a balanced and comprehensive code of moral conduct and holds that a clearly defined moral code, apt to uphold the dignity of all individuals in a just society, alone can guarantee peace, unity and security.

The top European thinkers of our time have started acknowledging that Western civilization has sacrificed the notion of morality in its hot pursuit of material progress, resulting into the emergence of a lop-sided society at the global level. Dwight D. Eisenhower, ex-president of the United States, once commented on the situation in these words:

> Our affluent society rests on shaky moral grounds. We reach the moon and pollute the earth. We long for peace and go war. An age that has split the atom must heal the splits in humanity. Empty hands must be filled with work, empty stomachs with food, and empty hearts with satisfaction. To cure the moral crisis that blights our world, each of us need only look to ourselves. If we each listen to the still small voice of conscience, we will soon perceive that simple basis things, like goodness, purity, unselfishness, love, integrity, are our greatest and most precious treasure. Seek affluence in these, and the tragedies of misused material affluence will end in happiness for all."[75]

---

[75] Sayyed Mujtaba Musavi Lari, *Western Civilization Through Muslim Eyes,* translated by F.J. Goulding (Qom: Foundation of Islamic C. P. W., 2008), p. 50.

5. Are all humans equal?

A claim of human equality defies the very philosophy of evolution. Evolution teaches that *Homo sapiens,* as we call the present generation of humans, has arrived the present stage by competing with its rivals, as the law of survival of the fittest tells us, and therefore, competition, not cooperation, is the law of nature. In this situation it is the power of a species to win against other species by suppressing them that counts in evolution and progress, not the adoption of a policy of equal rights for all to coexist and care for one another.

Islam teaches that all humans are descendants of Adam and deserve equal rights. It says that in practical life there may be differences among human beings in terms of gender, race, color and the like, but as human each individual and each community deserves equal respect and cannot be discriminated in any form. Islam makes an individual conscious of the rights of others on him or her and identifies those rights as *Huqooqul 'ibaad* (Rights of Others). Any sacrifice to uplift a down-trodden is greatly appreciated in Islam.

6. Can a developed nation force an underdeveloped community into servitude?

The evolutionists believe that as the process of evolution operates by the principle of the survival of the fittest, a developed nation has a natural right to consider an undeveloped nation or community as inferior and force it to serve its interest, or remove it from its way if its presence becomes cumbersome. *Neanderthals*, which were a species of humans, were (at least according to one theory) wiped out to extinction by *Homo sapiens* simply because it happened to be superior to *Neanderthals.* This could easily be traced to our time as well. Hitler unhesitatingly announced the superiority of the German race and fought for it and Europe and America practically follow it under the garb of the superiority of race or civilization. Harari writes: "But science was also used by imperialists to more sinister ends. Biologists, anthropologists and even linguists provided scientific proof that Europeans are superior to all other races, and consequently have the right (if not perhaps the duty) to rule over them."[76]

Islam says that humanity cannot be divided on the basis of color, race, gender, caste, tribe or civilization, declaring one nation or community as superior and the other inferior. An advanced nation, race or community cannot be allowed to exploit in any form the other nation, race or community for its lack of development. The Prophet of Islam, who was an Arab, declared most explicitly that in Islam no Arab was superior to a non-Arab, nor a non-Arab was superior to an Arab. In Islam a person achieved superiority only by virtue of piety of character

---

[76] Harari, *Sapiens*, p.337.

(*taqwa*).[77] Islam formulated its societies, culture and civilization on this very principle to the extent that even the slave dynasties rose to the position of rulers who were duly accepted by all sections of Muslims, a historical achievement in which Islam stands alone.

7. Is war essentially a virtue?

Evolutionists argue that as war is based on competition and provides an opportunity to the fittest for survival and dominance, it is a natural phenomenon and has to be appreciated as a positive fact of life. Harari writes that from the standpoint of evolutionists "the human experience of war is valuable and essential." He says further: "War allows natural selection free rein at last. It exterminates the weak and rewards the fierce and the ambitious."[78] The Western powers which have fought wars like the First World War and the Second World War have done so in the name of self-defense, a civilized way of renaming survival of the fittest. They justified them as "just wars," subjugated their 'inferior' competitors and celebrated their emergence as "superior" powers in the world. They now justify the production of the weapons of

---

[77] See the Prophet's Address delivered at the Farewell Pilgrimage (*Hajjatul Wida'*).

[78] Harari, *Homo Deus*, pp. 296-97.

mass destruction so that they could remain superior to their military competitors.

Islam wants to stop war at any cost and give peace a chance. It encourages Muslims to stand for peace even if they have to make a sacrifice for it. The Prophet of Islam practically did so when he signed the Hudaibiya peace treaty with the Makkans in which he accepted unjust, even humiliating, demands of the Quraish in the hope of bringing peace to the region. However, if despite sincere efforts to avoid it, a war breaks out, Islam instructs its adherents to fight "for establishing peace" by winning the opponents into the fold of justice and fraternity, as the Prophet of Islam did on the occasion of the conquest of Makkah. As Karen Armstrong acknowledges, "Muhammad took Makkah without shedding a drop of blood .... None of the Quraysh was forced to become Muslims .... Single-handedly, Muhammad had brought peace to war-torn Arabia."[79]

8. Will the human race destroy itself at its next evolutionary stage?

Evolutionists say that as evolution is a continuous process and as *Homo sapiens* is not the last species in the continuum of evolution, *Homo sapiens* will keep on evolving and produce a

---

[79] Karen Armstrong, *Islam: A Short History,* London: Phoenix, 2002. p. 20.

more powerful species which will be superior to *Homo sapiens*, but too different from it to be called human. It will be so different from *Homo sapiens* physically, intellectually, emotionally and morally that we will have to identify it by a new name, say, *superhumans*. Two things are clear: one, as evolutionists envision, "there seems to be no insurmountable technical barrier preventing us from producing superhumans,"[80] and, two, *superhumans* will be superior to *Homo sapiens* in all respects. At this stage a question will naturally arise as to how *superhumans* will deal with *Homo sapiens*? Will they ignore them and let them perish with the passage of time? Or will they enslave them and use them as guinea pigs, say, for experimentation? Or will they get rid of them once for all to ease the burden of the earth? The decision then will be in the hands of the *superhumans*. And as they will be following the rule of competition, in all probability they will not be kind to *Homo sapiens*. As Harari speculates, "it [bioengineering] would very likely bring down the curtain on *Homo sapiens*."[81]

Islam, on the other hand, accords the highest honor and dignity to humankind. It revolts against the slightest suggestion of a disgrace to humans, not to mention the wholesale genocide of the present race of *Homo sapiens*. In fact, the prime objective of human beings in Islam is to create

---

[80] Harari, *Sapiens*, p. 452.
[81] Harari, *Sapiens*, p. 453.

a society in which all live to celebrate the benevolence of God together. Sayyed Mujtaba Musavi Lari delineates a picture of the ideal society that Islam wishes to create:

> Islam's philosophy reverences the whole man in his world setting. It orders society's material behavior and benefits, while at the same time legislating for moral virtues, spiritual perfections, and a higher standard of living. By this it means, not simply the material, but the mental, the spiritual, the moral, the altruistic, the philanthropic standards which enable all men to live each for all and all for each.[82]

9. Can Western civilization plan a safe future for humans?

Evolutionists say that as life has come into existence as a result of certain blind natural laws and is functioning under their deaf and dumb governance, it has no set direction to go and no purpose to fulfill: "Evolution has no purpose."[83]   And because evolution sees no purpose in life, Western civilization, which is inspired by the notion of evolution, does not cherish a clearly defined purpose in life, certainly not a noble purpose. All it cares is the material gratification of humans. It, therefore, has neither a natural urge in it to create an ideal

---

[82] Lari, p. 64.
[83] Harari, *Sapiens*, p. 165.

future for mankind nor an ability to do so. Harari writes: "Yes, as best we know, microorganisms have no consciousness, no aim in life, and no ability to plan ahead."[84] This leads us to the conclusion that *Homo sapiens*, who are being governed by the law of evolution, will not be able to create a safe future for mankind, no matter how much resources it succeeds in accumulating with the help of science and technology. Harari affirms it in these words: "Science is unable to set its own priorities. It is also incapable of determining what to do with its discoveries."[85] This is of course also true about evolution.

Islam acknowledges that humans have a noble purpose in life to build a society which grants everybody a fair chance for full and free growth and self-fulfillment. Islam does not accept a position that humans are, as evolutionists say, being pushed forward by the blind force of evolution over which they have no control. Islam does not encourage humans to try to become god by conquering the material world; it calls them to become 'believers in God' who respect others and learn to live together in peace and love. It teaches people to cooperate, not compete to defeat others in order to maintain their superiority. It makes humans responsible for establishing an ideal society in which goodness prevails and wickedness is rejected so that people could enjoy bliss of togetherness. This is the prime objective of Islam and to establish it in the

---

[84] Harari, *Sapiens*, p. 446

[85] Harari, *Sapiens*, p. 305.

practical form on earth is what it considers the prime objective of humankind.

FIVE

CONCLUSION

We have discussed in detail important differences between Western culture and Islam in relation to our main thesis concerning the issue of the future of humankind. In this section we will try to conclude the discussion by emphasizing three points which will help the readers assimilate their thoughts and come to a conclusion about the issue involved.

First, due to overemphasizing material and intellectual aspects of life and ignoring moral and spiritual aspects, Western civilization is bound to become unbalanced, fragmentary and lop-sided. It is certain that the individuals raised in Western civilization will be materially affluent, but morally and spiritually pauper and will suffer from an internal conflict and a sense of incompleteness. Also, the society and culture that will emerge under its patronage will be devoid of selfless love, mercy, kindness, and benevolence.

Islam, by emphasizing the comprehensive value of material, intellectual, moral and spiritual faculties in humans, will create an individual, a society, a culture and a civilization which will be balanced, wholesome and free from conflict to the maximum extent. In an Islamic culture experience will be valued, but not at the cost of innocence, reason will be given due importance, but not by discarding imagination, scientific truth will be utilized for adorning the material world, but not by denying 'revelation,' individual gratification will be duly emphasized, but not by sacrificing social justice. A sincere effort will be made to achieve a synthesis and maintain an equilibrium, as far as practicable.

Second, as Western civilization refuses to take guidance from a higher authority (because it rejects religion and believes in the blind process of evolution), it at heart feels responsible to none and consequently does not hold itself responsible for planning a safe future for humankind: this future, it believes, will be automatically determined by the evolutionary forces that are controlled by the law of nature. That is why there is little hope that it will ever make a serious effort to correct and change its course of action. Harari points out this inherent problem in Western civilization in these words:

> . . . despite the astonishing things that humans are capable of doing, we remain unsure of our goals and we seem to be as discontented as ever. We have advanced from canoes to galleys to steamship to space shuttles – but nobody knows where we're going. We are more powerful than ever before, but have very little idea what to do with all that power. Worse still, humans seem to be more irresponsible than ever. Self-made gods with only the laws of physics to keep us company, we are

accountable to no one. We are consequently wreaking havoc on our fellow animals and on the surrounding ecosystem, seeking little more than our own comfort and amusement, yet never finding satisfaction.

Harari comments on the seriousness of the situation in these words: "Is there anything more dangerous than dissatisfied and irresponsible gods who don't know what they want."[86]

In Islam, on the other hand, the ruler as well as the ruled accept the supremacy of God to Whom they are answerable, and, therefore, they feel obliged to behave in a responsible way and work for the good of all. Islam promises to help humans achieve a life of freedom of thought and action, but it blocks all avenues through which an irresponsible person or a group may become a threat to the society. Islam encourages humans to attain happiness, but it forbids them from becoming slave to hedonism. It calls humans to attain moderation and achieve equilibrium in life which minimize tension, conflict and contradictions. This kind of life is possible, assures Islam, when humans promote the concept of collective happiness with a realization that God is watching. The faith in the omniscience and omnipresence of God and in the Day of Judgment makes them responsible as well as contented, assuring them that the achievement of justice is possible in the divine scheme of life.

---

[86] Harari, *Sapiens*, pp. 465-66.

Third, in spite of its glamor and buoyancy, Western civilization is negative in approach and instils a chilling fear and frustration in humans. It loudly announces its scientific achievements, but has no qualm in declaring that the next stage in evolution will in all probability witness the annihilation of the race of *Homo sapiens*. That is not all. The protagonists of Western civilization feel thrilled at the prospect of this new stage in progress and want all others to rejoice it. Atul Jalan concludes his book *Where Will Man Take Us?* with these words: "This is a beginning, not the end./ Behind us is Homo sapiens./ Before us is a whole new species./ We are the transitional generation./ What a great place and time to be in!"[87] Isn't it a call to *Homo sapiens* for mass suicide, telling its members to welcome it whole-heartedly as it would mark a higher stage of evolution?

This is where evolution will take humankind. But if we evaluate the situation in the light of the revolutionary progress in the field of science and technology, we again have a strong reason to feel desperate. Even if we leave aside the psychological impact of the threatening material structures surrounding us from all sides and instilling in us a feeling of man's insignificance that Dr. Alexis Carrel so ably discusses in his famous book *Man the Unknown* (2016), there is a genuine fear that the machines of tomorrow may go out of the control of their human masters and enslave them. We may ignore this

---

[87] Jalan, p. 273.

apprehension by reasserting our confidence in the superior power of humans, but this apprehension is potentially viable and the danger too serious to be ignored. These future machines will be so fast, so superior in intelligence and inherently so independent that after a stage their human creators will be no match to them; in fact, the whole world will be at their mercy. As we quoted Jalan earlier, the computing ability of quantum computers "would be equal to that of millions of conventional computers."[88]

In contrast, Islam is a religion of hope. According to Islam, humans are not only the best creation fully equipped with needed faculties to run the world in accordance with the will of the Lord; they also enjoy God's special love and mercy: "Do not despair of Allah's mercy." (Qur`an, 39: 53). There is a whole set of rules of check and balance which controls the individual as well as the society, but it exhorts humans never to lose hope in Him. As they are taught to fully trust God and believe in the wisdom of His judgment, they comfortably accept all situations, favorable and unfavorable, and live in peace. As a result, they have an inner strength, a strong morale and a conviction that they are born to change the world for the better. This difference between Western civilization and Islam creates two different kinds of mindset which will lead to the creation of two different kinds of world.

---

[88] Jalan, p. 41.

It is now up to us to decide which of the two will be a safe place for humankind to live.

BIBLIOGRAPHY

English

Ahmad, Ziauddin, *Influence of Islam on World Civilization*, New Delhi: Adam Publishers, 2006.

Armstrong, Karen, *Islam: A Short History*, London: Phoenix, 2002.

…………………………, *A History of God*, New York: Ballantine Books, 1994.

Bon, Gustav Le, *The World of Islamic Civilization*, translated into English by David Macrae, Spain: Tudor Publishing Company, 1974.

Briffault, Robert, *The Making of Humanity*, London: George Allen & Urwin, 1919.

Bucaille, Maurice, *The Bible, he Qur`an, & Science*, Delhi: New Crescent, 2012.

Carrel, Alexis, *Man the Unknown*, Mumbai: Wilieo, 2016.

Drapper, John W., History of Conflict between Religion and Science, www templeofearth.com.

Ebadur Rahman, Shah (Neshat), *Islam: Architect of a Progressive Civilization*, amazon.com (also on kindle).

…………………………………………., *Is Islam a Violent Religion?* Amazon.com (also on kindle)

Harari, Yuval Noah, *Sapiens: A Brief History of Humankind*, London: Vintage, 2015.

……………………………., Homo Deus: A Brief History of Tomorrow, London: Vintage, 2017.

Hitti, Philllip, *The Arabs: A Short History*, Washington, D. C., Regency Publishing, 2013.

……………………………., *21 Lessons for the 21ˢᵗ Century*, London: Penguin Random House, 2018.

Ibrahim, I. A., A Brief Illustrated Guide to Understanding Islam, Houston, Darussalam, 1997.

(*The*) *Indian Express* (Daily), "Synthetic Biology," Delhi, 18 April, 2019, p. 15.

(*The*) *Indian Express* (Daily), Delhi, "Meet 'virtual human' NEON, Tuesday January 14, 2020, p. 13.

Jalan, Atul, *Where Will Man Take Us?* Gurgaon (India), Penguin Random House,2019.

Lane-Poole, Stanley, *The Moors in Spain*, New York: Wallachia Publishers, 2015.

Lari, Sayyed Mujtaba Musavi, *Western Civilization Through Muslim Eyes* (trans. by F. J. Goulding), Qom: Foundation of Islamic C. P. W., 2008.

Mohsin, Syed Hamid, *Follow Me: Muhammad*, Bangalore: Salaam Centre, 2013.

Rao, Rama Krishna, *Muhammad: The Prophet of Islam*, New Delhi: Madhur Sandesh Sangam, 2016.

Walt, Montgomery, *The Majesty That Was Islam,* London: Sidgewiek, & Jackson, 1974.

Wells, H. G., A Short History of the World, New Delhi: Fingerprint Classics, 2017.

Urdu

Nadwi, Sayyid Suleiman, *Seeratun Nabi*, vols. 1 & 6, Azam garh: Darul Musannifin, 2011

Rahmani, Khalid Saifullh, *Inquilab*, the Urdu daily, Delhi edition, Monday, August 29, 2016.

Usmani, Muhammad Taqi, *Tawzihul Qur`an*, Delhi: Faisal International, 2017.

Zafar, Mahmood Ahmad (Hakeem), Shah Waliyullah awr Unke Tajdidi Karname,

INDEX

www.ingramcontent.com/pod-product-compliance
Lightning Source LLC
Chambersburg PA
CBHW020737160726
47993CB00006B/2491